Who Am I Today?

Poems of Identity Crises by Steve Gerson

Spartan Press

Spartan Press

Kansas City, MO

spartanpress.com

Spartan
Press

"Deftly delivered, elegantly crafted, the volume subtitled 'Poems of Identity Crises' cements Steven M. Gerson's rank at the forefront of contemporary American poets. Timeless, yet evocative of our troubled present, *Who Am I Today?* opens with gorgeous odes of great, requited love. Section by section, bridged by apt quotes from literary masters, it then radiantly encapsulates the travails of immigrants amid xenophobia, women confronting misogyny, veterans grappling with PTSD, and individuals facing anxiety, infirmity, and mortality. This is Americana writ large with the dream/idea/promise beset by harsh, enervating reality in a land of mass deportations, male chauvinism, memory lapses of soldiers' sacrifices, and economic spoilation alongside unfathomable wealth. But no matter the subject matter, the luminous language employed by this Poet Laureate of the Everyday, of the American 99.99%, elevates one's spirits, quiets tension, and provides hope regarding humanity's fate."

-Dr. Robert C. Cottrell, author of the forth-coming *The Heyday of Willie, Duke, and Mickey: New York City Baseball's Golden Age Amid Integration.*

"Who Am I Today? is a poetry chapbook that showcases the vast array of human experience and emotion. It captures myriad facets of human identity, the highs and lows of love and heartbreak, the dichotomy between inclusion and exclusion, the hope of youth and experience of age, the bloom of health and the withering of the infirm. Whether these poems offer readers explorations of the familiar or insights into new territory, they'll resonate with all and leave them thinking and wanting more."

-Stacy Harken, JD, Information Architect/ Technical Writer, Garmin Industries

"Steve Gerson's eighth book of poetry brings to the reader his deep feelings about relationships and social justice as embedded in the natural human process of self-reflection and self-actualization. As Steve begins all his books with a poem dedicated to his wife, Sharon, *Who Am I Today?* presents a longer selection that speaks to not just love but meaningful connections and the dedication one feels through a strong, long-lasting relationship. Consistent with his latest books, Steve's observations about justice and human caring emerge thematically, especially with the early poems reflecting the value of immigration to our culture. When seeking to understand 'self,' as the title suggests, Steve readjusts his writing from historical perspectives to the human soul. Embracing his love for nature expressed through metaphor and imagery, he shares insights with harsh realities affecting the human condition as described in 'Travel's Travail' and 'In this time of anxiety.' Taking the human condition to the maximum, 'Existential Cataract' reflects on aging and life change—a natural order. This latest collection speaks to the mind and soul of the reader while reaffirming that as a living society, we are all just humans seeking to understand our role in a very complex and confusing world. Steve Gerson helps us answer our own question: Who Am I Today?"

-Bill Lamb, Ph.D.

Acknowledgments

"Who am I Today," *Panoplyzine*

"Semaphore\Distress," *In Parentheses*

"Refugee," *The Antonym*

"Teeming Shores: a Triptych," *God's Cruel Joke*

"!not," *The Rainbow Poems*

"?Goddess," *New Words Press*

"Soundless Screaming in the Nothingness of Your
Space," *In Parentheses*

"woman suffocating under skyless clouds," *Variant*

"Woman at the Edge," *Antonym*

"Divorce Proceedings, Case #2029," *In Parentheses*

"Modern Romance," *Scapegoat*

"Love/Loveless," *The Bookends Review*

"The Girl with a Tattooed Heart," *WildSound*

"breathing underwater . . . a Vet returns to Norfolk,"
NOVUS

"PTSD," *Dillydoun*

"Posted," *Panoplyzine*

"God and Country," *Two Timbers Press*

"A Truck in Snow," *Zoetic Press*

"Photo Album," *Vermilion*

"Screamscape," *Vermilion*

"3 a.m.," *Indolent Books*

"In this time of anxiety," *Scapegoat*

"Self Portrait as Angst," *Wingless Dreamer*

"Tattooed straight lines not sufficing," *In Parentheses*

"Submerged under Eclipses," *God's Cruel Joke*

"Self Portrait as Hologram," *Panoplyzine*

"Stars Aching under Distant Skies," *Down in the Dirt*

"Addiction," *Down in the Dirt*

"Hank in Hospice," *CafeLit*

"Dementia," *In Parentheses*

"Through Darknesss," *Wingless Dreamer*

"Existential Cataract," *Gasconade Review*

"The Plaintive Moan of a Dry Man," *Wingless Dreamer*

"Phantom," *Online Journal of Arts and Letters*

"A ·ban ·don," *In Parentheses*

"Still Life," *Panoplyzine*

Table of Contents

Introduction

Who are you? Is your identity in crisis? If so, no big surprise there. Times are stressful, and we're in flux.

We're defined (he/she/they? BIPOC? LGBTQA? Cisgender? Us vs. Them? Old vs. Young?), but who are we with and without others' expectations? How do we reflect the multiplicity of our personas? How do we manage our diverse identities?

This chapbook provides a cross section of our times, as seen through the prism of identity challenges.

For Sharon, as always

If I had none

You say my head is full of words,
some rhyme, some sputter and smear
like grease popping on a hot stove,
some rise in updrafts as birthday balloons,
many fall like raindrops onto already
sodden grass too wet to absorb, and
I'm left with muddy shoes, but
I never have enough words to describe
you.

So I keep writing, poem after poem,
year after year, like pages in a spiralbound
tablet, turn the page, turn the page, I've
got more to say—you're inexhaustible to me,
my love for you as long as a sentence composed
of every word in Webster, plus a thesaurus, plus
Shakespeare's canon, plus the lyrics for tunes warbled
by the world's birds, continent to continent, and
still I have more to say.

If I had no words in my head, if I couldn't borrow
     words
from poets or priests or paleontologists excavating
     words
from ancient palaces, somehow I'd approximate
words to tell you of my love, maybe seashells to

> decorate

my thoughts or leaves in the fall to dance my love or
clouds to paint pictographs of passion or fruit for you
to taste the sweetness of my heart or fish to swim
> ballets
of love or air to breathe my care into your ear or just
> my hand
tapping subliminal messages on the small of your
> back,

if I had none.

Who Am I Today?

Prologue

Who am I Today

Yesterday I needed
to be strong a gull
flying against gale
headwinds buffeted
by wind shears grayness
graying in turbulence
she was hurting and
I needed/wanted to
be wings

Last week I was
weakened in the face of
24/7 scirocco newscasts
hurling blisters like
sandstorms arid epithets
of dissension divisiveness
and I leaned on her
she a palm tree rooted
in an oasis of heart

Last year amid viral
wasps stinging with
spores amid the contagion
of TikTok influencers
earworm drilling vlogging

blogging I was a reeling
tweetstorm a mental
hurricane of barometric
upheaval

Tomorrow I'll invent
my next self my next
sense of being needed
to confront the whatever
life invites a new
roiling endemic an
old familial relationship
requiring massaging
I'll knead plead reseed

I Am Immigrant

"A nation, like a tree, does not thrive well till it is engrafted with a foreign stock."

-Ralph Waldo Emerson

Fractal

You think you see me
walking through a checkpoint
know me through geometry
gauging distance
between my eyes nose lips chin
plotting a fractal faceprint
I barely see myself
in mirrors reflecting mirrors
versions of me
me v. 1.0, v. 2.0
standing between parents
deceased behind me
like migrants disembarking
in Kodachrome sepia
like immigrants seeking
trespass through barbed wire
saguaro thorns slicing memories
before me generations
blooming a cataract future
myself a hologram quavering
a light field lightly drawn from multitudes
all speaking tongues to sealed ears
waving arms as semaphores to shuttered eyes
but you think you see
my infinite dimensions

Semaphore\Distress

! We hold down
created (un)equal
gender specific
endowed rights
(? self-evident)
that ~~all~~ certain men
are ~~inalienable~~
pursuing life
(! can't breathe)
liberty
happiness
among others with
in\justice on their throats:

Refugee

Leaving tree shards, gray streets,
Cadaverous cement, skeletal girders,
Julietta Uskyavic arrived, June '89,
To a land green with promise.

Homeless, tempest-tossed
Words unfamiliar fell upon her as suffocating leaves,
Skies as corn blue as her Kosovo flag glared,
Sunlight cast shadows.

Julietta, transplanted,
Saw unseen,
Heard unheard,
Touched untouched.

Below Deck

I am an American, because my grandparents suffered through a voyage below deck. They roiled in tempests. They ate grub-infested cornmeal. They traveled without an itinerary other than any land would improve their prior status as second-class field workers digging potatoes out of rocks. What would await them? Open arms or thrown epithets, hope or hunger, an America the beacon or shores lashed by waves of hate and distrust? They arrived. They struggled. They thrived. I was born into the country they helped to build, one meriting their dreams. I take my democracy for granted, the democracy they achieved by rising from below deck.

Seagulls seek updraft
to rise above turbulence.
Wings reach horizons.

Travel's Travail

Imagine the travel to freedom.
Imagine the travail,
crossing dangerous seas
in dingy boats, overcrowded
with fear, the wailing of wonder
at one's destination, then land,
beset by ruthlessness as biting
as concertina wires, hunger as
empty as pockets defrauded
by hopelessness stealing hope,
then walls to breach as impenetrable
as language barriers, followed by
coyote screams, teeth tearing holes
in cloth threadbare as want. Maybe
you reach the dream. Maybe you
find a home in a new land that
casts a guarded glance, questioning
your right to happiness and you
settle into security. But deportation
lurks like a gallows' shadow, like a
vulture swooping in a black gyre, like
a machete singing the air in a hiss. You
celebrate safety but fear the noose of
immigration. Imagine the travail of such travel.

Teeming Shores: a Triptych

1. What it must

What it must have felt like to land on our shores a
dark sea behind them dark clouds of oppression
dissipating like a swarm of bees the hissing
becoming silent and now
just open skies a land waiting to be tilled my
grandparents arriving with an
alien language of consonants and only hope
filling their baggage now reoccurring
daily at our borders new Americans wanting to
quench their thirst and breathe air
without bombs with the unlimited opportunities
of limitless horizons what it must feel like

2. Camino Real

Roberto y Isa walked weary through saguaro
thorns past coyote screams and dry gulch
bones broken dreams of hope scorched in heated
air casting mirages on the sand of
freedom sought like water in empty canteens
toward the Camino Real a royal road
over a wall of anger a shout of wrath shredding
like concertina wire into Eagle Pass
and there on new land saw a future that opened
like air intake on breath-wary lungs

3. **Departing**

She left the boat from Haiti sailing on a 20-foot
skiff to Jamaica sea-washed salt-sodden
with a Coke bottle of fresh water and cooked
cornmeal wrapped in plantain leaves
hunger as constant as fear she and 22 others
barefoot ragged Levis she and her infant
daughter tied to her bosom as tightly as a dream
then migrated to Arizona its heat an
incubator for her future where she built a life but
long blue arms entered her church as
she knelt in prayer the arms hauling her toward
deportation her dreams departing like
heat waves shimmering in mirage

I Am Her

"Being born a woman is my awful tragedy. . . .
I want to be able to sleep in an open field, to travel
west, to walk freely at night."

-Sylvia Plath

!not

going to: follow your punctuation rules
for who you think, I am, today

a pink (gauzy) syntax
in your red/state white/male cataract

no!t going to be pastel
quiet interrupted a grl

mascara my (im)perfection wear froth
to slake your thirst your hand

holding my throat like a beer bottle
?want me to dress like something edible

a pomegranate pansy whirl of cotton candy
to sweeten teeth not going to

bend under your shard ceiling bend over
ogled an *objet d'*morsel fckd

on your testosterone timetable accept 7/10th
of a dollar my X boxed in [by your y]

not going to stay in line pirouette on cue
stand on blistered toes to reach higher

dance for your reality show government
, can't, won't:

?Goddess

!No

Goddess in your kitchen?
Isn't this good enough? I'm balancing
pots and pans while teetering
on the stiletto tip of your pointed barbs.

Goddess in your bed?
Isn't this good enough? I'm wearing
the peekaboo negligee from your
XXX online purchase.

Queen of your checking account?
Ensuring that you haven't overspent
your budget for nonsense, unused, who
wants/no one wants.

Strutting the catwalk of your fantasies
while you flaunt, flout, fuck the cutie
from the bar, the TSMatch (yeah, I saw
your online history).

Tending the pooch you wanted,
tucking you into your ego, being the
significant other (what? When am I
significant?) you need at the moment

you need a partner—supper, sex, an ear to hear
your tales of self. And I smile and I nod and I
coo and I ooh. That's me, a pat of butter frying
in your heat; me, skydiving, oxygen-deprived

in your atmosphere; me, pages in your book,
unbound, my words struck through by your edits,
redacted; me, a pail, hole-punched, leaking.
In your selfie, I'm off center, out of focus.

And I'm screaming,

!No

Soundless Screaming in the
Nothingness of Your Space

When you stole into the room like an eclipse,
your halfmoon eyes hiding behind the
asteroid crashing, I knew what you'd say, saying,
"I'm seeing someone else," my feet unearthed,
zero gravity free fall swallowing my screams
soundless in the nothingness of your space.

woman suffocating under skyless clouds

bovine in her way
dressed uniformly in muddied russet
glazed cow-stare straight
like vacant windows in farm outbuildings
black as eyeless sockets

she endures self-stockaded
as if muzzling stray blades
of grass on barren browned fields
downward gazing under leafless trees
every day a late fall

not always so numbed
she once effervesced
I recall her eyes uplifted yearning
after passing planes flying elsewhere
contrails etching sun-streaked paths

but life intervened siloing her
a romance denied her moans lowing
a career curtailed cowering
friendships family all plowed under
climate changes in her soul

till tariffed by slights her sights low
she ruminates suffocating under skyless clouds

Woman at the Edge

Each day before dawn
Maria Olvidado reached for the sea
To escape her husband's fists
His knuckles roughened by her bones.
      Each day the sea's undertow stared.

Each day before he rose
Exhausted from ministering
His *tequila* stewed justice
She asked the sea for answers.
      Each day the sea's undertow stared.

Each day before returning to *marido*, Hector
She cleansed in the sand
Reddened from sunrise
She appeased in the sea's mist.
      Each day the sea's undertow stared.

Each day before the next day
Maria sent Hector's nightly bottle
To sea, sailing it to fathom
The sea's destiny on a distant beach.
      Each day the sea's undertow stared.

Divorce Proceedings, Case #2029

Barometric pressure twisting between invective and
indifference, he, for her, was like breathing the hot
dry air of Arizona, scalding, his heat an acetylene
torch in her throat, like breathing swamp humidity
in Louisiana, each breath breathless, so her lungs
strained, gasping like a beached fish, gill quivered.
Loveless, his arms withheld from her as if he were a
Greek statue lopped limbless by marauding infidels
stealing her belief. She had tried standing tall on
Doric columns, their filigreed flutes and fillets her
fragile strength, but he, like seawater salt, like acid
rains, eroded her resolve into fissures, and she, as glass
blown in fire and air, a bowl to carry water, blue as
sustenance, stream fed, shattered under his burden,
water evaporating into rock dry sand.

Modern Romance

She wore toxic mascara.
It scribed her face in icicles
when she cried, often.
She filed her nails
into penknives to carve
down his back, his chest, his arms, his face
in romance, in anger, as often.
He bathed in Agent Orange.
It wafted from him as mephitis
from sulfurous sinkholes.
His pointed, steel-toe stingray
boots, sharpened on acid,
bit into her with each embrace.
They married when the wind
screamed, guests applauding
their divorce.

Love/Loveless

Act 1. You and me

Filets of trout perfectly browned in warm butter
beside a quartered lemon slice on two Wedgewood
plates. A carrot-sculpted rosette. Two glasses of rosé.
Brown, yellow, blue, orange, red passion. "I'll have
iced tea; she'll have water." The server left us alone
to hold hands in the flickering light of a candle, the
shape of light caressing your face like breezes rustling
a redbird's feathers.

Act 2. Her

I just want someone. Why can't I find someone? They
come in here every week, sit at the same table, hold
hands, never see me, see only each other, like I'm a
distant noise, a car crash in some other neighborhood,
a solar flare whose eruption won't affect their climate-
controlled environment, a damned iceberg calving,
dissolving into the sea, disappearing into atoms small
enough to be carried on the waves of their love sighs.

Act 3. Me

You caulk the seams between my stone edges and your
seamlessness. You are chocolate drizzled on my finger to
lick. Let my thumb inscribe circles on your palm to plot
roads we'll travel. Let my tongue touch your tongue and
speak of time and song.

Act 4. You

You help me see light in different colors. The other
men I've known have been as cataract, their needs
obscuring my vision of self. "Come on, babe, just
this once, I promise." "Hey, get me a beer, won't ya',"
he'd say while scratching his lazy ass. "Let me tell
you what I think." "That chick friend of yours has
a big mouth, always goin' on about her this or that.
I mean, who gives a you know what?!" You listen.
You take the words I speak and weave them into
garlands.

Act 5. Her

Four more hours of this shift. Burning my hands on
hot plates, my soul searing in loss. Then what? An
empty night of Hulu. Bottles of Bud diesel clanking
against my teeth, the sound resounding throughout
my hollow apartment. Endless loops of "Beautiful
Pain," Eminem screeching in AK-47 staccatos,
"Yesterday was the tornado warning/Today's like the
morning after/Your world is torn in half/. . . It's like
an enormous asthma."

Those two, sitting at the table, eyes fondling each
other, their hands linked like a bridge joining his
hemisphere to hers.

I'm falling, my gravity gone and I'm reeling into ether,
nothing tethering me. Loveless. I want. And my
want echoes.

The Girl with a Tattooed Heart

2:36 a.m.

"I want," she wrote in her laptop journal, her fingers pecking at the keyboard like a bird seeking seeds. "I want sunshine. I want robins, daffodils, parades with balloons, a glass of red wine over a candlelit dinner. I want to hold someone's hand," as ice droplets froze on her bedroom window. She picked up her handheld from the nightstand to read his text, again. "This isn't working, Jen." Four words after their eight months together. In the second month, she said, "I think you're the one, Jim." He smiled and nodded. At the fourth month, she said, "I love you, Jim." He smiled and nodded. At month seven, she asked, "What can I do, Jim?" He shrugged and looked away. She wondered why she wasn't enough. She wondered how else she could have made him happy, as she tugged at the bandage covering her left forearm, her nails bitten and bloodied around red cuticles. She pried one edge of the gauze up and pulled it from the scabs of her newly inked arm, decorated with a heart and two initials, J & J. Jen read his four-word text, again, then she turned off the handheld and shut her laptop, the light extinguishing like a flower closing. The ice on her window started to melt in rivulets like exclamation points.

2:47 a.m.

I Am Veteran

"The only thing harder than leaving a friend behind in combat is coming home and knowing that they didn't come back."

-Tim O'Brien

breathing underwater . . . a Vet returns to Norfolk

from the overlook   wind flowers
          the tufted marsh reeds
reefed by crab dunes   as undertows weep
                    the shoreline
into uncertainty
          salt scouring illusion

low clouds turn gray   fraught with green mist
          caught in an upswell
                    from heavy surf
and the rumble   of distant lightning
surges like pulse
          in deepening   seabed churn

breath underwater bursts sand bleeds blistering

PTSD

I hear the buzz of starlings swarm
And cloud the sky in blackening drear.
Their fearful clattering in harm,
Their murmurations shriek and warn
My empty house cloaked in fear.

Each day the thousands pale and fail.
They die like shredded shrouds tear
And curtain my mind's wail
While plagues of garbled voices rail
My empty house cloaked in fear.

Wars uncivil, terror flights,
Fists uplifting in despair,
The urge to love succumbs to fight
The right with words, the wrong with might,
My empty house cloaked in fear.

It's chattering of starlings crazed.
A man goes down as truncheons rear
In blood and bones and faces dazed.
Broken beaks shredding unphased,
My empty house cloaked in fear.

Posted

"he wrote the postcard," she said,
her head held low in her hands,
her knuckles white, her eyes red,
"right before shipping out to the Middle East,
posted to who knows wherever Anbar is,"
he wrote, "tell you more later babe, gotta go,
we're climbing in our C-17 transport from
Naval Base San Diego, me and my squad
taking off over the ocean, the sun reflecting
like an invitation, my sarge joked, more like
hazard lights to me, but what do I know,
a grunt coming from nowhere Silent Knife,
Oklahoma, biggest body of water I'd seen
that pond in your grandpa's back 40, I can see
the lighthouse we visited up on the hill overlooking
Point Loma that day you wore blue gingham,
the color of your eyes, the color of the Pacific
at dawn the day I asked you for your hand,
me kneeling like some damned picture show star,
you laughing, a smudge of lipstick on your teeth,
you my girl then and now and forever" the card
arrived almost a year to the day after he was reported
KIA, delayed by bureaucracy, postmarked "Dead Letter
Wash, DC" she kept the postcard on the fridge
pinned like a bug in biology class and read his last line,
"see you soon, hon," the words thumbed and fading

God and Country

The grate at 8th and Main breathed warm air
against the December cold so I claimed
it as home unfurling my newspaper
sheets reporting Dow gains and cardboard bunker
unpacking my random cans and jug of
Johnny Red next to my camo backpack
my pinned purple heart hanging like clotted blood

I had fought for land before as squad leader
3rd Marines Desert Storm leading 12 men
toward smoke and sand commanding resources
not sufficient for a resume so fighting
for God and country led to life under bridges
and food foraged from dumpsters I lie on
the grate my face etched from metal like strafing scars

A Truck in Snow

He parked the truck beneath the oak behind the barn
across the lake then handed the keys to his younger
brother Hank with a backslap and wink, walked to her
and said, "Don't worry, Beth, I'll be fine, you know me,
always careful," and hugged her, kissed her, and turned
toward the road, a bus waiting.

2004, spring, the oaks in bud, starting to leaf out. He
was off to Iraq, they said, but who ever really knows.
Once on the bus, he waved to the family through fly-
speck windows, they waving back, and he was gone, dust
pluming on the country road. Beth wrote daily, at first,
and waited.

No news, but the family said, "He's busy, probably, girl.
He'll write when he gets a chance," and spring became
summer. The truck sat beneath the oak, baking in the
Kansas heat, the sun radiating off the truck's red panels,
the truck's hood pinging in the heat, like a heart beating.

She wrote weekly, her time taken up with chores, and she
waited, and she was pregnant. No news, but the local
paper reported heavy fighting near Al Anbar, where he
was maybe stationed, so the family said, "stay calm, Beth.
He's involved. He'll be fine. You know him, always
takes care." In autumn, the leaves fell, littering the truck
with pastels, leaves stuck to the truck's windows like
lost letters. Beth wrote weekly, mostly, but sometimes a
month would go by.

No news, and she was 5 months and showing. The house was heavy with quiet. No one in the family talked about the war, anymore. When winter hit, snow covered the truck, covered the oaks, covered the barn, iced the lake, and the farm was iced in fear, like nighttime chills.

The baby was born after that first snow, a boy they named after him, his father gone to war. Another truck stopped by the house later that winter, and a man got out. He tugged down his khaki dress uniform jacket, straightened his tie and hat, and looked toward the house with downcast eyes, eyes that were tired from telling tales before. He plodded through the snow with heavy boots. Before he knocked on the door, Beth opened it, the baby on her hip, her eyes starting to redden like his truck in the snow, buried in cold.

News had finally arrived.

Photo Album

I found it in the attic,
behind the armoire,
cobwebbed in darkness
and time, a photo album
faded as Kodachrome and
loss, and on the pages,
slanting askew from yellowed
paste, I saw my father.

He stood in a row with other men,
waiting. They wore starched uniforms
in Navy white, bad haircuts, skin showing
above their ears where hair had hidden
the sun, fists held tightly in anxious hands,
and ashen faces. The world was at war.
He had enlisted with hope and fear and ancient
duties to ideals grown like midwestern wheat.

I never met him. I was born 27 days after
his death at Pearl Harbor, 16 days after my
mom heard a knock on her door and saw two
men in starched uniforms, their eyes downcast.
I couldn't feel the flames he felt. I couldn't breathe
the water he inhaled. I couldn't hear his screams
as he sunk along with the Arizona, his flesh
on fire, his dreams deferred like winter wheat
　　threshed.

Decades later, I stood as he had, my haircut as
bad, my uniform as starched, my fears agitated as
propellor wash. I wouldn't board a ship at Pearl.
I trudged through sand in Iraq, IEDs awaiting
each step like vipers, bodies exploding to repel an
enemy's 9/11 attack. My troop had taken photos,
too, one day to be stored in darkness. We stood in
line, young men pretending strength, waiting for
sacrifice to ideals. From the album, I felt his eyes,
his past overlaying my present like a specter of
    prophesy.

Screamscape

Can you tell me about your dream?" the VA hospital psychologist asked.

Dream, I thought. Not quite the word I'd use. Dreams always implied wishes and cotton candy and big-ass red Corvettes and Tahiti and tiny umbrellas in coconut drinks and beautiful babes and children flying kites in April and money. I wasn't having dreams.

Each night for the past eight months since out-processing, leaving Afghanistan, shedding the heat like sheep sheared of their winter coats, seeing the sand diminish from the DMZ like time lost, the portholes of my transport plane misting in misery, I landed in nightmare.

Here's what I had earned in my tour of duty: Sergeant's stripes stitched on my sleeves, a purple heart hung around my neck, PTSD pinned to my chest like a service medal, and night terrors buried in my brain like IEDs stuffed inside a dog's carcass.

Each night, I'd hear the howls of shattered bones sprouting from the desert like death totems, see blood dripping from splintered words spoken through mouths of broken teeth, taste the smell of cordite sizzling torrid air, feel my fingernails ripping through hope like skin shredding on concertina, touch shrieks of cluster bombs dappling my conscience like hypodermic needles. And see them, victims of war. The men beside me on dirt trails that wound like intestinal coils through cold mountains. The villagers who saw our presence as ghouls, eating their valleys like flesh.

Each night my head screamed. Each night I turned my sheets into wet gauze, encasing my body in surgical bandages. Each night my eyes blared red like sirens. Each night my blood pulsed through my veins like rotor wash. Each night I woke shouting dead men's names, this my Cocteau Rimbaud screamscape. Each day I feared the next night.

After waiting for a response, the psychologist asked again. "Can you tell me about your dream, Sergeant?"

I reached into my back pocket for a handkerchief, raised it to dab at sweat pocking my forehead like shrapnel, brought the cloth down quickly to wipe away a tear I hoped the doctor had not seen, and said, "No. I can't remember anything."

I Am Anxiety

"Oh the nerves, the nerves; the mysteries of this machine called man! Oh the little that unhinges it, poor creatures that we are!"

-Charles Dickens

3 a.m.

I see evening all day, 3 a.m. every hour,
and the day's night sounds like dissonance,
a dream distorted to blue and black.

In the nightly day, I run fearful streets,
looking back on crows flying crooked
through slanted air, a house with vortex windows,

the door a jagged maw, a dog moaning, its flaming fleas
dancing a derelict jig. Heat sizzles into cold, expiring
on darkness like a moon's corona behind a constant cloud.

In this time of anxiety,

I hide. From the fear. My fear of fear.
Fear of touching. All those virus-besieged
canned goods in the grocery stores. I'm
scrubbing my hands with antibacterials.
Wearing two masks. Fear of touching
you, too. Will you respond? In kind?
Will you recoil? As if I'm virus-besieged?

Fear of commitment. To you. To my
current job. Not a career, just a job.
My IDP asks, "What do you want to achieve
this year? In five years?" I might as well
write my plans on sand, on a beach, at high tide.
I might as well write my life plans on Snapchat.
Deleted after 30 days if/when unopened.

Fear of failure. Or success. Fear of wars.
Even peace is frightening, because then
I should be happy, right? Fear of high prices.
Fear of forest fires and floods and hurricanes
and mortgages and tribal politics and my car breaking
down and a tooth cracking when I have no dental
coverage and rogue dogs and road rampages. Fear
of fear.

Don't even mention cyberattacks on my already low
credit card rating by Russian hackers demanding
cryptocurrency ransoms. I've never committed a crime.
So I fear police will stop me for some minor infraction.

"6:00 p.m. News Flash: man shot while failing to change
lanes correctly. Police report that he wasn't obsequious
when questioned."

So I hide.
Fearfully.
With my pulse ratcheting.
Like seismic spikes.
Under fault lines.
And I quiver.
With one eye peeking.

Self Portrait as Angst

1. Specters come and go

That's me on the table pinioned
by angst, my tendons ripped and tied.
I'm sipping ether narcotized
and looking at an Xray of my evisceration.

Or maybe I see instead I think a reflection
in the surgery room's halogen lamp,
hot as the eighth circle of hell, my lies of self,
and specters come and go, clothed in bones.

I know I'm somewhere in the blackness of the
        room
between the twisted corners and shadows listening
at the edges of my sight. Maybe that stain of paint
dripping down the wall like needle tracks.

I'm dressed in old stanzas from another person's
        poem,
ill fitting. A Rimbaud tie, the waistcoat Apollinaire,
one sleeve Poe, the other Cocteau. And Duchamp
        shoes worn
on my hands to warm my soullessness.

2. Stirring my bile with a wetted finger

I look down upon my flayed self to see my heart
pumping like teeth tearing   teeth   teeth
   teeth   teeth
each tooth a spike on the heart rhythm monitor
   gnashing
at the worm of my stringed pink intestines coagulating.

Crouching over me, a monocle-eye reflects
my skull, drawn and cornered as in jailcells
above the cancelled corpus of thorned
crowns, miniscule pink flecks pitting like petechiae.

And then the silence of a resting drill,
its whirr awaiting the bite. I dream myself
escaping down wayward streets,
deserted as dust-sawn limbs.

I bolt upright from the gurney's straps
and roll my sleeves up, my arms tattooed
with liver spots, scrivener's glyphs
demarking my experience without innocence.

3. Crows and buzzards

I am no Bartleby preferring not;
I have supped gluttonously at last tables,
Iscariot, and mouthed ill words
and swallowed untruths whole

and watched for mermaids riding
unicorns but saw only murderous crows
and a wake of buzzards circling skies
ingesting war-torn babies' cries,

And now the end, Byzantium,
my hair thin, my eyes glazed, words
on a page through fractal trifocals
as hazed as worms, slithering maggots

wriggling on a pin. I want to eat a peach,
a pear, take bites of apple cores fallen
from snake-infested trees and pray for forgiveness,
but I see a tunnel darkening and no hand of God.

Tattooed straight lines not sufficing

I will ink my face
like Queequeg's living parchment
a hieroglyphic labyrinth of enflamed
etchings so that looking in a mirror

inverted I can rewind my past searching
each swirl an undertow an eddy churning
an aspiration exclaiming dead ends and
blurred attempts my trail of overlapping

incisions testing truth one line intersecting
with another serpentine circumnavigating
cutting off/into paths of maybe
where stop starts the journey's wander

for me to draw meandering moments
not in red desire green need blue despair
yellow lust blotted smudges of ink leeching
into pores and worn fissures a map of maladroit

missteps like scrimshaw totems each pit scar and
facial flourish a glyphic inflection in transit
but black and white finality decisively unraveling riddles
of heaven in earth then perhaps I could find my way

through straight lines a linear treatise my face a poem
a grid pole star aligned but this maze I see reflected
reflects myriad fractals more surely the passage of chaos
in ink unspooling

Submerged under Eclipses

Drowning in her laptop monitor, streaming Hulu horror shows, she wept dry tears. Her anxiety, red as fear, boxed in her heart racing like minnows from kingfish, each beat a shiver of terror, her chest a constricting cage, her breath heaving for escape. And she scratched welts on her bare arm like eel teeth.

"Why?" she asked, more a shriek than a moan, a groan more than a scream, as if her angst bubbled up from being submerged in sludge, a life trudging through want.

Each day, today, last week, tomorrow, she darkened, the darkness creeping on her skin like kelp wavering in the doubt of cold currents.

Sometimes her fears unsealed and she saw relief. She breathed breath in ease. And the sun shone, though clouds gathered in the east, a distant thunderhead building with serrated edges.

"Yes, I'd like that," she cooed when asked to meet. "Yes, I can be there at 8:00," she demurred, though 8:00 was late for her needs. "Yes," she said, though she meant "no," her voice muffled as if under waves. "Yes, that's ok, if that's what you'd like," she said, looking for an exit, her eyes darting like bait fish from predators.

But, often, too often, undertows appeared, bruise-colored, blue-black, deep in panic, darkness again, the hole opening to emptiness. And she'd sink, grasping at options that tore her fingernails ragged as hope.

And the day became night, always. And she swallowed
eclipses.

Under water, breath burns.
Sight blurs in cataracts.
Blue blackens in depth.

Self Portrait as Hologram

Bam. Bam. Bam. Loud knocking on my door.

"Hey, you! Sam. I know you're in there.
Open this door, you hear me?"

Half in, half out of my apartment's third floor window,
I started to climb onto the fire escape to avoid him, the
super, not having paid my rent this month, again, for
the fourth time in six months, due to having lost another
job, my third in a row, if you force me to be honest.

The latest HR dude said in the exit interview, "You're
neither here nor there, are you? More absent than present,
more exit than arriving. Just a no-show in general, huh?
We feel like we hired a fleshless phantasm, an aura of
irrelevancy, an apparition of indecipherable angst, a sort
of 3-D person, more spectral interference than substance.
When we asked your colleagues about your work
ethics, they said, 'Who?' We couldn't find anyone who
remembered working with you. All I can say, Sam, is
good luck." Then he ushered me to the door.

So here I am, in ether, not in a building, not on the
ground, just hovering in midair, this time on a rusted,
rickety fire escape barely bolted to my tenement's
crumbling, 50's, post-war brick facade. I'm swaying. I'm
wavering. Light beams from the surrounding buildings
are reflecting through my nothingness.

I'm looking down at the weeds smothering the building's facade. As an expert on imbibable analgesics, you know, booze, I see relief, the glinting telltale signs of broken beer bottles, shards of glass sharp as scalpels honed against the rough edges of my anxiety. "A few stab wounds, a stinging laceration might help. I'd rather be a mess of self-injury than what I am now, a hologram."

> *Through the open door*
> *Motes drifting in death spirals*
> *The empty room screams*

Stars Aching in Distant Skies

2:47 a.m.
Distant skies are aching.

A locomotive's lonesome
whine weaves between

the Cuyahoga hills.
Voles fleeing foxes skitter

in the undergrowth outside
my bedroom window,

then a silenced scream, bones
crunching. The spigot in my

bathroom drips, its rhythm
the beat of a Hank Williams song.

I'm lying in bed sipping on a Chivas
to numb my ache. The night weighs

on me like stars extinguishing, sizzling
as cigarette butts thrown into my

near empty liquor glass.
The locomotive will quiet

soon to an absent moan,
lost in the dark hills, the train

heading toward the track's end.
2:47 a.m.

Recipe for Anxiety

Want to eat some stress? The simple recipe for anxiety starts with living now, in this era, this existential moment of divisiveness, peppered by a past president, a Putinesque tyrant, and ample dollops of fear.

Add to those horrors the following essential ingredients for Anxiety Stew:

1. Obtain 1 lb. of emaciated polar bear steak by trolling through rapidly melting ice floes.

2. Slice the meat into strips and then using baton-wielding police brutality, pound the polar bear meat into compliant tenderness.

3. Cube 3 cups each of carrots, potatoes, and onions, then radiate these vegetables through global warming by placing the cubed ingredients in your kitchen window.

4. Season the meat and veggies to taste as follows:
- 1 heaping tablespoon of salt tears from Ukrainian losses
- ½ cup of pandemic-induced flop sweat
- ¼ teaspoon of antibacterial hand sanitizer
- a whiff of panic from cyberattacks and cryptocurrency ransom demands

- 2 pinches of jiggling Kardashian clickbait
- 1 soupcon of oxycontin for flavor

The result: a blood pressure of 170 over 110, a heartbeat of 96, hives, a headache, and a perpetual grimace as you grind your fists into your temples.

Share the results of your anxiety stew with an Instagram photo, write about your worry in a snapchat post, and join millions of other 21st century survivors by posting on social media this recipe of our common ailment—stress.

Reeling

it looked to be I thought I knew
what appeared to seem a cause
for care or maybe just today's
phantasm cloud shearing cover
for yesterday's uncertainty

so I took a breath to control
my (dis)courage and stepped up
to face life saying I can meet
these tsunami swales of 24/7
social media blasts of newscasts

decrying my political choices
my shopping habits my gender
identities the foods I eat the gasoline
I waste the greenhouses I destroy
the loved ones I (dis)trust and disappoint

oh come on! I'm reeling
in confusion a dirigible
untethered enflamed and immolating
an avalanche cascading suffocating
my mind a phrenologist's map

of conflicting dementias psychotic eruptions
I've bitten my tongue numb in blathering
(mis)communicating with doppelgangers

seeing double like Picasso's girl before a mirror
placing my right hand on my left shoulder

my right eye staring dumbly at my left sty
and all I want is footing but no!
what I have is migraine hallucinations
mirages dissipating in heat waves
cataract conclusions myopic miseries

stop! this world on its skewed axis
is tilting roiling foiling spoiling, and I'm tired!

I Am Infirmity

"Bear with my weakness. My old brain is troubled.
Be not disturbed with my infirmity."

> -William Shakespeare, *The Tempest*,
> *Act IV, Scene I*

Addiction

I need.
I'm boiling from the inside.
My skin is crevassed with
volcanic eruptions.
My tracks map Odysseus'
tortured trek from Troy to Ithaca,
beset by witches and beasts and
a god's curse. I'm feeling like a man
wracked in the trenches
of Dante's 8th circle, wanting.
Ravished with tattooed skin glyphs
swarming like locusts in Exodus,
a biblical plague assaults my body.
But then the pin prick of juice slithers
into my veins like a melody of fire,
and I swirl into an oblivion of ice.

Through Darkness

1.
Like
bats'
night flight,
fear hiding
behind thorned brambles,
cloud-shrouded penumbras aching,
the pronouncement arrived: cancerous lesions
    amassed.

2.
A
gasp,
shudder,
reckoning
of fearful import,
How life changes in instances.
Shadows engulf like ingesting lunar eclipses.

3.
Then
what?
Chemo,
gasoline
slithering through veins
like venomous coral snake fangs
piercing, shrieking, victimizing, dehumanizing.

4.

Now

what?

Ripped, marred,

seamed, stitched, scarred.

Breath. Life suffices:

self received through ignominy,

self retrieved from coiled snakes, melted bones,

    lightning struck nights.

Hank in Hospice

Bedridden, infected by COPD, coughing spores like
spring weed blossoms spewing seedlings, an orchestra
of atonal allergens, I'm lighting my Pall Mall Reds,
unfiltered, watching the smoke tendrils weave graveside
garlands as ashes sift downward in gyres of despair.

"How ya doin', Hank?" my caregiver asked. "Can I
bum one of them cigarettes from ya?" He lit his off
mine, the two burning butts meeting in conflagration
near the third circle of hell.

I coughed again, my phlegm orchestrating new
disharmonies as wheezes crackled through my lattice-
worked lungs, my face sallow, the color of parchment
soaked in nicotine, the color of cheap rye whiskey,
my eyes red-rimmed, looking like a miner's pit glowing
ravaged fire.

"How am I doing you ask?" taking a deep drag of tar
and terror. "I'm bedridden. My cheeks are sunken
like a truck hood, hailstorm-dented, rusting in a used
car lot and some fool has put a sign on me saying,
'Barely Runs, Good for Scrap.' I'm dust. I'm sifting
toward perdition, and I wish the chariot would hurry
up and get here. That answer your question?"

Dementia

At first my pauses were commas,
synapses between now and next,
uncertainties, ellipses waiting
for closure, my mind only partly
cloudy with sunlight seeking sky
like a sentence ending, expecting
the next capital letter, but in time.
stops. lingered. longer. longing.
Now, my gauze-eyed gaze brackets
air; my words stumble in syntax
shards, muffling screams; my steps
stutter shuddering like inverted
exclamation points¡¡¡

Existential Cataract

I had my eyes checked today.
It seems I've seen life through
cataract lenses all gray

and distracted, my periphery
dim my distance contracted
in shadows with edges myopic.

My soul's a corneal hole distorted
from what's rosy and pure
as if on day one of creation

my DNA missed the memo
about light's expiation
from darkness. So I've stumbled

past colorless mores. I'm all sties
of stigma. What should be black
and white, you see, for those enlightened

has degenerated my cataract
topography. I've become a
fathomless depth of moral opacity.

The Plaintive Moans of a Dry Man

Thou exists on many a thousand grains that issue out of dust (Measure for Measure, Act 3, Scene 1)

I'm old. I'm dry. The marrow in my bones
moans like Mahler's plaintive flute.
My walk stumbles with brittle hips.
I shuffle in small steps, hesitant to meet
what's cowering beyond the corner
hedge turning brown in a dusty sky.
My eyes see blurred through cataract
haze, words wriggling on pages like
casket worms. Sound comes to me as
crow coughs from a dark mound.

I reach to turn the doorknob with palsied
hands, fingers crooked as question marks.
Why have we surrendered to evil, history
smoldering in charred pages, the predator
teeth of war raking children's innocence?
Why have we stopped our ears with ignorance,
humming banalities that allow tyrants to walk
upright from their coiled nest of serpent sleep?
Why am I shrinking from your touch,
from the sun, seeking shadows?

What slithers from the edge like
an eclipse of fear, darkening our days?

Our crimes hang from wrath-wrought trees
like plums rotting in impudence, the plum pit
stuck in my throat like doubt. All around I see
feathers molting from starlings, their black
iridescence shimmering in accusations. All
around I see rose bushes black in decay. All around
I see vanity of vanities, blackening in broken
mirrors, my fingers shredded from glass shards.

And in this depraved month of my dry age,
my dry brain, my dry tongue bleeding on words
as ragged as assonance, gulf winds blowing
warning signs red and black, the spider's web
unraveling as worried syntax, I and you and we
and us are tenants of condemned homes.
We are ghosts of what could have been.
I am lost in time's tumult of broken bones.
I am dust, blown as from a god's hand,
nonchalantly.

Phantom

1.
Trails
of
sawdust
dementia
termite ridden
his mind losing time
a rusting structure eroding
and what was once a man became empty edifice

2.
Not
all
at once
slowly as
crosscut tree rings gnawed
exposed to toxic DNA
and what was once a man became nubs, whittled splinters

3.
A
house
foreclosed
keys returned
what a man became
when losing his identity
inch by inch like an amputated leg's phantom pain

A ban don (əbandən)

Noun: My room was dark in abandonment

Adjective: An abandoned Christmas tree,
hospice-delivered but forgotten,
leaned against a corner void
to my right. No tensile streamers.
No string of colorful lights.
Dry needles littered the floor,
thirsting.

Verb, past tense: Ambient light
like a lost guest seeped in through
the window to my left. A dim glow
had abandoned the wintery gloom,
sun setting behind disturbed
clouds reflecting gray snow.

Noun: I could hear but not see cars
speeding with abandon, their whoosh
the sound of my intubation wheezing,
heading rapidly toward a hazy destination.
Minutes before, my caregiver had read
the chart hanging from my bed like an
amputated foot. "How are you?" he asked,
but his phone interrupted.

Verb, present participle: He held up one finger
in pause, said, "Got to get this. Be back soon,"
before he left the room abandoning me to silence.

Adjective: From my window, I saw a skeletal
cell tower, out of service, no reception. An
abandoned grocery cart, wheel-deep in snow,
sat empty in the cold field, wind whistling through
it as a marrowless bone flute to awaken specters.

Noun: I was dark in abandonment.

I Am Mortal

"Because I could not stop for death — He kindly stopped for me."

-Emily Dickinson

Fear

I'm frightened

maybe it's age
and I fear the thread
I've pulled is near
the end of its skein

I'm frightened

maybe it's mortality
and I fear the fraying
of synapses like a
bridge out in high water

I'm frightened

maybe it's regret
and I fear
the holes I've jabbed
are spilling water

I'm frightened

maybe it's uncertainty
and I fear that tomorrow
will punish time
like a cat toying with prey

I'm frightened

but my fears are
unrelated to age
infirmity or disease
what I fear all I fear

is life without you

Self Portrait in Bone

What does this ossification tell,
our tale of skeletal stories?
Our smallest bones, the hammer,
the anvil, the stirrup,
jangle through our canals,
reaching our phalanges to tap toe
in rhythm; our largest bones,
femur and tibia, become war
clubs in cannibal hands.
Our shoulders broad loads of sorrow
and success, only to be broken
by the hubris of scalpel-thin scapula.
Sinners and saints, devout and deviant,
we pelvic thrust in rapture
and rapaciousness.
Our marrow hollows into peace pipes
or a satyr's flute of deviltry.
Yes, we fly the moon, craft concertos,
cleanse oil-slick seabirds, and sculpt
our likenesses as gods, attempting to
stand upright in societal mores,
but our vertebrae surrender, hinged serpentine.
We slither into slander and slaughter.
Our ribs encompassing breath become
merely air, wind chimes in death,
where moans wail as sciroccos through
desert canyons. The orb that crowns our

brainpans, filled with miracles, empties of ideation
like a basin draining into drought-dry dirt.
Our organs depart. Our songs stop singing.
Skeletal, we are heartless.
Pulverized, our bones paint a self portrait in ash.

Still Life

death is up for interpretation
my soul squandered in a grave

your bones rattling in an October
mansion accompanied by screams

my identity emptied like a hypodermic
needle flushed into subcutaneous flesh

your self excised in flagellation
skin flayed like an orange excoriated

or maybe in death we find lost love
our temporal egos shed naked from

femur to fibula scapula to sacroiliac
earthly degradation removed like tongues

dissolved lies no longer spoken our brainpans
empty as books without words so the essence

of emotion can emerge in rhythmic script
or death allows for uninhibited orgies in

Dante's second circle our bones playing like
tempanis wind blowing through our marrow

in devil's horns perhaps the sacrament of denied
sentience sins expiated to become one who believes

in afterlife. No. Bones can reject death's pride.
Bones can embrace sacrilege to fear no evil.

Internment, worms, charring? Use my ashes instead
to paint a composed still life in vibrant gray.

Alternative Realities

1. Threadbare, Perhaps

"How you doin', Marie?" she asked, ignoring
the more pressing questions, like since Jim died,
since the kids moved from Abilene to God knows
where, since Marie's life had become as empty
as a drained Coke, can crushed and tossed in the
dumpster.

"Ha," Marie laughed like air seeping from a
flattened tire. "I'm working at the thrift store off
23rd and Elm." She paused, pushing a strand of
thinning gray hair behind her right ear. "It ain't
too bad, three days a week, minimum wage and
commission, given my limited work experience
and my GED, having left school at age 17,
pregnant with little Johnny. I get to see people's
failed dreams. Clients come in with their used
and torn clothes, hoping for a big consignment,
then get paid 25 cents on the dollar. Customers
come in, checking all the coat pockets for a lottery
ticket, hoping for a big win. Then they find lint."

"What's next, girl?" she asked.

"Yea," Marie laughed again, this time like a
wind chime blown off a tree branch onto drought-
dry dirt. "That's the question, ain't it. What's
next?" Marie removed her glasses to wipe a
smudge from a cracked lens. Life holds its secrets

close like a dollar fortune teller at the state fair, turban askew, crystal ball purchased wholesale online. "I know what I'm doin' this afternoon," she said cryptically.

Marie would visit Jim. She'd weave through the headstones like a needle sewing threadbare cloth leaving holes that couldn't be fixed, stand over his marble grave, imagine him in his pine coffin, his right arm lifting up like a tentacle to draw her down into his coffin's embrace.
Marie had a plan.

2. Regift, Perhaps

"How you doin', Marie?" she asked, ignoring the more pressing questions, like since Jim died, since the kids moved from Abilene to God knows where, since Marie's life had emptied like an apple tree, all its fruit plucked in the Fall.

"Ha," Marie laughed like air filling a flat tire. "I'm working at the thrift store off 23rd and Elm." She paused, pushing a strand of thinning gray hair behind her right ear. "It ain't too bad, three days a week, minimum wage and commission, given my limited work experience and my GED, having left school at age 17, pregnant with little Johnny. I get to see people dream. Clients come in with their used and torn clothes, hoping for a big consignment then whoop when they get found cash. Customers come in, checking all the coat pockets for a lottery ticket, hoping for a big win. Sometimes they find a stub just waiting to be reclaimed."

"What's next, girl?" she asked.

"Yeh," Marie laughed again, this time like a wind chime dancing in spring breezes. "That's the question, ain't it. What's next?" Marie removed her glasses to wipe a smudge, pausing to clear her view. Life holds its secrets close like a dollar fortune teller at the state fair, turban askew, crystal ball purchased wholesale online. "I've got the start of a plan," she said cryptically.

Marie would visit Jim. She'd weave through the headstones like a needle sewing threadbare cloth, renewing its tatters, making the remnants pretty much good as new, stand over his marble grave, and remember his gifts: love, kindness, care.

Around his gravesite, Marie saw the winter's brown grass turning green in the beginning of Spring.

Epilogue

Multitudes

Weaving, warp and woof,
Identities spooling as
Quilted multitudes

Dr. Steven M. Gerson, Professor Emeritus, Johnson County Community College, Overland Park, KS, was named 2003-2004 Kansas Professor of the Year, chosen by the Carnegie Foundation. He is the co-author, along with his wife Sharon Gerson, of 13 college-level textbooks and the author of seven poetry chapbooks: *Once Planed Straight: Poetry of the Prairies; Viral: Love and Losses in the Time of Insanity; The 13th Floor: Step into Anxiety; And the Land Dreams Darkly* (Spartan Press-KC); *There is a Season* (Online Journal of Arts and Letters); and *What Is Isn't*. He has published over 400 poems in many journals and is honored to have been named a finalist three times for the North Dakota State University Press Poetry of the Plains and Prairies award. Steve is most proud of his 55 year marriage to Sharon, for whom all his love poems are written, his wonderful family of Stacy, Stefani, Rob, Bobby, and for the joy of spending time with his three grandchildren: Sophia, Samantha, and Jacob. These people are the poetry of Steve's life.

This project was made possible, in part, by generous support from the Osage Arts Community.

Osage Arts Community provides temporary time, space and support for the creation of new artistic works in a retreat format, serving creative people of all kinds — visual artists, composers, poets, fiction and nonfiction writers. Located on a 152-acre farm in an isolated rural mountainside setting in Central Missouri and bordered by ¾ of a mile of the Gasconade River, OAC provides residencies to those working alone, as well as welcoming collaborative teams, offering living space and workspace in a country environment to emerging and mid-career artists. For more information, visit us at www.osageac.org

Osage Arts Community